Tell Me about When Moms and Dads Come Home from Jail

also in the Tell Me about Jail series

Tell Me about When Moms and Dads Go to Jail
Judi Goozh and Sue Jeweler
ISBN 978 1 78592 807 9
eISBN 978 1 78450 842 5

of related interest

The Boy Who Built a Wall Around Himself
Ali Redford
Illustrated by Kara Simpson
ISBN 978 1 84905 683 0
eISBN 978 1 78450 200 3

Can I tell you about Loneliness?
A guide for friends, family and professionals
Julian Stern
Illustrated by Helen Lees
ISBN 978 1 78592 243 5
eISBN 978 1 78450 526 4

How Sprinkle the Pig Escaped the River of Tears
A Story About Being Apart From Loved Ones
Anne Westcott and C. C. Alicia Hu
Introduced by Pat Ogden
ISBN 978 1 78592 769 0
eISBN 978 1 78450 669 8
Hidden Strengths Therapeutic Children's Books series

The Healthy Coping Colouring Book and Journal
Creative Activities to Help Manage Stress, Anxiety and Other Big Feelings
Pooky Knightsmith
Illustrated by Emily Hamilton
ISBN 978 1 78592 139 1
eISBN 978 1 78450 405 2

Trauma is Really Strange
Steve Haines
Art by Sophie Standing
ISBN 978 1 84819 293 5
eISBN 978 0 85701 240 1
...is Really Strange series

Tell Me about When Moms and Dads Come Home from Jail

Judi Goozh and Sue Jeweler

Jessica Kingsley Publishers
London and Philadelphia

All images reproduced under the terms of the Creative Commons Attribution 2.0 Generic license with thanks to the photographers.

Page 10: David Dennis, Flickr

Page 11: Ben Seidelman, Flickr

Page 14: Pierre Tourigny, Flickr

Page 15: Jennifershwalm, Flickr

Page 16: heymarchetti, Flickr

Page 17: Tamckile, Flickr

Page 18, left: verkeorg, Flickr

Page 18, right: USAG – Humphreys, Flickr

Page 19: Lucélla Ribeiro, Flickr

Page 20: Carissa Rogers, Flickr

First published in 2018
by Jessica Kingsley Publishers
73 Collier Street
London N1 9BE, UK
and
400 Market Street, Suite 400
Philadelphia, PA 19106, USA

www.jkp.com

Copyright © Judi Goozh and Sue Jeweler 2018

Front cover image source: 123RF, iStock and pxhere. The cover image is for illustrative purposes only, and any person featuring is a model.

Library of Congress Cataloging in Publication Data
A CIP catalog record for this book is available from the Library of Congress

British Library Cataloguing in Publication Data
A CIP catalogue record for this book is available from the British Library

ISBN 978 1 78592 806 2
eISBN 978 1 78450 843 2

Printed and bound in China

We dedicate this book to the children with an incarcerated parent and their families, who struggle each and every day, and to the professionals who are dedicated to helping them through difficult times.

We also dedicate this book to our families—our husbands, Paul and Larry, and our children and grandchildren.

Acknowledgments

Our journey on behalf of children with an incarcerated parent has been guided and supported by many. In 2007, our mentor, Art Wallenstein, who was the Director of Maryland's Montgomery County Department of Correction and Rehabilitation, made it possible to create a project to raise awareness about this often-overlooked and underserved population. Robert Green, as warden of Maryland's Montgomery County Clarksburg Facility (MCCF), offered great support as well. Kendra Jochum, LCSW-C Reentry Services Manager at MCCF, worked tirelessly and made incredible contributions to this effort. Randall Wylie provided the important photographs from MCCF that show the reality of jail so that children can see the real-life, real-world situation for a parent. From the beginning, Dr. Craig Uchida saw the importance of this issue and offered us tremendous support and continues his own work for children with an incarcerated parent. Jeff Franklin and Archie Coates, creators of PlayLab, Inc., have been with us every step of the way to give our writing an appropriate visual format. Cindy Perlis, Director of *Art for Recovery* for the UCSF Comprehensive Cancer Center at Mount Zion, gave us her creative insight and guidance on these books.

James Cherry, Editor at Jessica Kingsley Publishers, Ltd., gave us a fabulous home for our work. His enthusiastic support for this book has been an inspiration. His warmth and professionalism have been stellar and we thank him for the opportunity to highlight issues for children with an incarcerated parent. Editorial Assistant Daisy Watt has shown patience and support throughout the entire process of publication.

To the Reader

This book will help you understand what is happening to your mom or dad who is working hard to come home after spending time in jail.

Tell Me about When Moms and Dads Come Home from Jail tells a story about a child like you who finds out that Dad is coming back home. You may have many questions about what will happen and, throughout the story, these questions are answered.

Moms come home from jail, too. Even though the story is about a child and a dad, the same story, questions, and answers are true for you when your mom comes home from jail.

You may have a lot of different feelings about the situation, from sadness, worry, and confusion to anger and not wanting to be with anyone. All your emotions are normal. Feelings are not right or wrong—they just are!

Tell Me about When Moms and Dads Come Home from Jail

When I came home from school, Mom was nervous and excited and said she had something to tell me.

She told me that Dad is coming home from jail. Dad has been in jail for a long time and I was a lot younger when he was last home. I miss him, but I am a little worried, and nervous, too. I wondered how we will get along. I wondered if he would be different. Would he still love me? A bunch of questions were swirling in my head.

When can Dad come home? Mom said Dad has to work on a Reentry Plan. He works with a person to figure out what he will need and come up with ideas to help him when he finally comes home and goes back into the community. When Dad's sentence is up, we can pick him up and bring him home. Some people can take a bus or taxi home.

What do "parole" and "probation" mean? Mom said that when Dad follows all of the rules and his jail sentence is almost finished, he might come home and live with us. He may need to be on parole or probation. I was curious about what that meant.

Mom said that parole is when a person like Dad is in jail; he can go back into the community but must continue serving his sentence under the supervision of a Parole and Probation Agent until the end of the sentence. Before he is released, he can earn "good days" and "work days," which will reduce the amount of time of his sentence.

Mom said that part of Dad's sentence might be probation, which would allow him to stay at home instead of going to jail. Dad could also get probation after his jail time. He will have to follow certain conditions and report to a Parole and Probation Agent, who might even visit him at our home.

Is it easy to come home after being in jail? I am really excited about Dad coming home, but I am also not sure what it will be like and I am a little scared and stressed out. I have learned that what happened to Dad is not my fault. I asked Mom what she thought. She said that Dad has been away from us for such a long time that he would have a lot to do in jail to get ready to come home. She said we all will have to make some adjustments.

She told me she was scared and that Dad was probably scared, too. I really hadn't thought about the way my parents might feel. She said it is okay to be worried and afraid, and that because we might all have these feelings it would be a good place to start to talk about it together. We could be each others' support

system. She also told me there were going to be good days and bad days for everyone.

When Dad was in jail, he had job readiness classes to help him learn how to search for a job and do a job interview. If Dad had a drug problem he would work on a treatment program to get off drugs and stay clean from drugs when he got home. When Dad gets home, he will need to work hard to get a job and work with the people and places that can help us if we have problems.

When Dad comes home, what can he do to help me?

Dad can:

- understand that Mom and I had a hard time while he was in jail
- use the good stuff he learned during his reentry classes at home with me and our whole family
- know that his mistakes are not my mistakes
- show me he can give himself a chance and create better avenues for himself
- listen to me about my thoughts and feelings
- talk to me
- respect me and my privacy
- be honest
- love me
- trust me
- make time to be with me
- help me with homework
- try to understand me
- do things together as a family like go to the movies, play games, and have dinners together.

What can I do to help my dad when he comes home?

I can:

- understand that life inside a jail is really different from life outside of jail

- understand that he may be overwhelmed when he comes home

- know that he wants to be in my life and I want him in mine

- love him and know he loves me

- listen to him

- talk with him and forgive him for our lost time

- try to express my feelings and let him express his

- try to be sensitive to his thoughts and feelings

- understand that if he does something I don't like, we all need to talk about it

- try not to be judgmental.

If I feel angry or worried or frustrated, what can I do?

I can do a lot of things to help myself:

- Talk to my mom or my dad.

- Talk to a counselor or teacher or clergyman or social worker or someone in my family or a person I respect and who has been there for me.

- Learn skills and strategies for controlling my anger and then use the strategies I have learned.

- Write about my feelings or even draw pictures.

- Listen to music.

- Read a book.

- Take a walk.

- Exercise.

What do I say to my friends? Mom said that some things in families are private. Our family can talk about them to each other and decide together who to tell and what to say. If my family says it is okay, I can talk to people I feel safe with and realize that some people can be judgmental, but other people can really help me.

What will happen in the future? Even though there are times when I am afraid, sad, confused, worried, and angry, I know that when Dad gets out we can be a family. I know that he has been working hard to change. I hope he won't get in trouble and leave our family again.

I know I am a good person. Dad made mistakes and wrong decisions, but that doesn't mean that I will. Whatever happens, I know I will be okay. Having Dad home will be a new beginning!

Activities for Children

Expressing thoughts and feelings through writing and drawing is helpful. Writing poems or stories or a collection of sentences and drawing pictures can be ways to share your feelings. Writing and drawing can make you feel less stressed and even put you in a better mood.

It might not be easy for you to say what you think and feel in a conversation. Writing and drawing are other ways you can share what is in your mind and heart.

Writing Activity

DIRECTIONS

If you wish, you can write about your ideas and feelings on a piece of paper or even keep a journal. You may write a poem or a story or the lyrics to a song or just some sentences. There are no grades when you write and it will feel really good when you can let people know how you feel or let them read the words you write.

Some Ideas You Might Want to Write About

- How did you feel when Mom or Dad came home?

- How is your life different now?

- I want my mom or dad to know_____.

- What do you want to say to your friends when they ask you about your mom or dad?

- What do you want to say to your teacher, counselor, clergy, or someone else important to you when they ask about your mom or dad?

- Make a list of what is bothering you and how you can feel better.

- Make a list of all the people in your life who can help you feel safe.

- Make a list of all the good things in your life.

- Make a list of all the things you would like to say to your mom or dad.

Drawing Activity

DIRECTIONS

If you wish, you can draw a picture about your ideas and feelings on a piece of paper. It is okay to only use color or lines to express your feelings. You may use symbols (like a sun or a heart) or stick figures. You can pick a color that describes your feelings and just color in the whole page. There are no grades when you draw and it will feel really good when you can show people how you feel.

Some Ideas You Might Want to Draw a Picture About

- This is how I feel.

- Draw a picture of your feelings (angry, sad, lonely, or another feeling) for your mom or dad.

- Draw a picture of all the good things in your life.

- Draw a picture of the activities you want to do with Mom or Dad.

Tips for Parents and Professionals

Introduction

A Department of Justice report from the year 2007 says that 2.3 percent of children in the United States (nearly 1.7 million children) had an incarcerated parent. In spite of the statistics, coming home is a unique and personal journey for anyone who has been incarcerated.

There are many factors to consider when a parent comes home. It is important to be sensitive to how the child reacted during the period of incarceration. It is important to consider how strong the bonds for that parent were prior to the incarceration and whether the child maintained any type of visitation or connection.

If you are reading this book, you have someone returning from jail or you yourself might be coming home. You need to be aware of how much the child might have changed during the absence of the parent. Basically, new bonds will need to be formed with all family members. In addition, the parent also needs to be aware of how they themselves have changed while away due to the environment they were living in prior to coming home.

With support, this can be a very successful reunification. We hope this book helps you to be sensitive to the needs of the child and that some of the activities will help create a positive experience for everyone involved.

If you are a professional or caregiver who is reading this book, we hope that the ideas and photos will encourage conversation between you and the child.

WHY USE THIS BOOK?
Kids Who Have a Parent Coming Home from Jail

- This book will give you honest answers about what happens when your parent leaves jail and comes home.

- This book may give you information so that you can talk to someone who can help you.

- This book will give you a chance to write about your feelings or draw a picture that shows how you feel.

Anyone with an Incarcerated Relative Coming Home

- This book will help you explain what is happening to the child's incarcerated parent, how to help the child, and what family members might experience when the parent comes home.

- This book will help you initiate a meaningful discussion with the child.

Professionals Who Serve this Population

- This book is a resource to use in conjunction with counseling, therapy, and any other services you offer to a child experiencing parental incarceration.

- This book will help you explain what the family might be feeling or wondering.

- This book will help you initiate a meaningful discussion with the child.

- This book will be helpful as a problem-solving activity.

HOW TO USE THIS BOOK

- Read the book.

- Look at the photographs.

- Think about the questions and the answers.

- Talk to a person about your thoughts and feelings.

- Write or draw about your thoughts and feelings.

- Ask any other questions you may have.

GUIDING DISCUSSION QUESTIONS FOR KIDS, FAMILIES, CAREGIVERS, AND PROFESSIONALS WHO SERVE THIS POPULATION

- What are you thinking and feeling because Mom or Dad is coming home?

- What are you worried or scared about?

- What would you say to a friend at school after your parent comes home?

- Would you like some help to talk about what you could say to your friends?

- Do you have any other questions?

Helpful Hints for School-Aged Children with an Incarcerated Parent

These are ideas that children and families may use as they navigate through the issues related to parental incarceration.

Children who have an incarcerated parent feel the same level of trauma as children who have had a parent die or whose parents have divorced. The children may exhibit aggression, defiance, disobedience, depression, anxiety, and/or withdrawal. Younger children may show withdrawal and anger, especially to the person taking care of them.

If there are many other losses, such as losing the income of the other parent, changing homes, losing friends, having to move, or having to live with a grandparent or another relative, then the child may experience even more behavior issues. Even if the child stays with the other parent, he or she may have to cope with social stigma, stress in the family, and, often, feelings of shame.

Sometimes the parent or caregiver is so overwhelmed with all of the issues they have to deal with that the children's needs are ignored.

School-aged children may have additional problems with school work and issues with their peers. They may be very reluctant to discuss their feelings and often maintain a facade that everything is okay. These same children may experience low self-esteem.

Research shows that school professionals can be critical in making sure that children who have an incarcerated parent are properly assessed and supported.

The following strategies may be helpful to the adult who spends time with a child who is impacted by the incarceration of a parent. Use this list personally or share it with someone who could benefit from the ideas.

- Ask open-ended questions that will not just be answered by yes or no. Some examples are:
  - › What are you thinking and feeling because Mom or Dad is coming home?
  - › What are the things that worry you?
  - › What would you say if someone at school or your friend asked you about your mom or dad?

- When your child talks to you:
  - › Try to be a good listener.
  - › Parrot back what your child says. For example:

    Child: I feel scared at night.

    Parent or caregiver: I wonder what you are scared about.

  - › Be aware of your body language:

    Make eye contact.

    Be aware of your facial expressions.

  - › Keep an open mind.

- When you talk to your child:
  - › Be honest.
  - › Be calm. Model self-control.
  - › Be patient.
  - › Be consistent about rules.

- › Encourage your child to express anger by using words.

- › Use "I Messages." For example:

  This is not an "I Message": You never clean up after yourself.

  This is an "I Message": I get upset and frustrated when I pick up your toys after you play with them.

- Tell the school staff personnel with whom you feel comfortable about what is happening to you and your family. Share the impact of the situation, especially if the child is acting out or displaying depression. (Talk to the counselor, teacher, principal, speech and language pathologist, special education teacher or case manager, or any other staff member with whom you are comfortable.)

- Talk to your family doctor or someone at your clinic or urgent care facility.

- Contact agencies or organizations for help.

- Find positive and healthy outlets for you and your child, such as helping others or keeping a journal.

- Foster a positive relationship between your child and the incarcerated parent.

For further information or comments and suggestions, feel free to contact us through our website: www.creativefamilyprojects.org

Handling Conflict

Conflicts happen in our lives. Triggers are the verbal and non-verbal actions that can start a confrontation with another person or group. In order to understand our triggers, we need to understand the warning signs and how we can recognize them in ourselves and others. We also need to understand coping mechanisms. They are the actions we can take to increase the amount of think time and cooling-off time between recognizing we've been triggered and taking an inappropriate action. Using coping mechanisms can change a negative response to one that is positive. In this way, conflicts can be avoided.

CONFLICT-RESOLUTION
Triggers

Verbal Triggers
Get out of my face!
It's your fault!

Warning Signs
Hands sweating
Heart pounding

Non-Verbal Triggers
Rolling your eyes
Holding up a fist

Mind racing
Red-faced

Reactions
Negative reaction

Coping mechanisms
Take deep breaths
Count to ten
Take a walk

Reactions
Positive reaction

ATFRC: ACTION/THOUGHTS/FEELINGS/REACTION/CONSEQUENCE

Each of us is in control of our behavior. We make choices about our behavior based on our thoughts, feelings, and motivations at the time. Changing our thoughts can lead to different feelings, reactions, and consequences. Developing this "habit of mind" can help create more productive resolutions to conflicts.

ACTION	ACTION
THOUGHTS	CHANGE THOUGHTS
FEELINGS	FEELINGS CHANGE
REACTION	REACTION CHANGES
CONSEQUENCE	DIFFERENT CONSEQUENCE

Example for understanding how ATFRC works:

ACTION	ACTION
The child picks up a book.	The child picks up a book.
THOUGHTS	**CHANGE THOUGHTS**
The child thinks, "It's my fault my dad went to jail."	The child thinks, "It's my fault my dad went to jail. Mom told me it is not my fault. Dad broke the law."
FEELINGS	**FEELINGS CHANGE**
The child feels angry.	The child feels sad.
REACTION	**REACTION CHANGES**
The child throws a book across the room and breaks a lamp.	The child puts the book back on the table.
CONSEQUENCE	**DIFFERENT CONSEQUENCE**
The mom punishes the child.	The mom sees that the child is sad and gives him a hug.

WHERE TO GO FOR HELP

- School counselors and teachers

- Social workers

- Pediatricians

- Community agencies, including Health and Human Services, Mental Health Association, Child Welfare

- Churches and other religious houses of worship

- Professional colleagues

- Additional, appropriate resources at the library or online

Resources and Further Reading

WEBSITES

The Annie E. Casey Foundation
Children of Incarcerated Parents Fact Sheet
www.aecf.org/resources/children-of-incarcerated-parents-fact-sheet
This fact sheet presents data on parents as prisoners, the affect this has on the children and how foster care plays a role.

Ensuring Success for Children with Incarcerated Parents
www.aecf.org/resources/ensuring-success-for-children-with-incarcerated-parents
This discussion guide shares statistics, solutions, and next steps for funders interested in aiding children of incarcerated parents.

Creative Family Projects, LLC
www.creativefamilyprojects.org
Creative Family Projects, LLC identifies problems and provides solutions by synthesizing information from organizations, institutions, and corporations into booklets and training modules for the benefit of children, youth, and families.

"Echoes of Incarceration"
www.echoesofincarceration.org
This film, produced by teens with incarcerated parents, intercuts the stories of four young people with the voices of experts and advocates in the field, and creates an emotional, compelling case for the importance of ongoing parental contact.

For Children in Foster Care

Partnerships Between Corrections and Child Welfare

www.aecf.org/resources/partnerships-between-corrections-and-child-welfare-collaboration-for-change

Partnerships Between Corrections and Child Welfare: Collaboration for Change, Part Two explores the gap between the systems, which results in tremendous hardship on children, caretakers, families and workers in both places, and what can be done to improve coordination without a great deal of additional funding.

Foreverfamily

http://foreverfam.org

Foreverfamily works to ensure that, no matter what the circumstances, all children have the opportunity to be surrounded by the love of family. The organization focuses on providing services to children with incarcerated parents and their families.

The National Resource Center on Children and Families of the Incarcerated

Download helpful materials for service providers and families.

Children of Incarcerated Parents Library

http://nrccfi.camden.rutgers.edu/resources/library/children-of-prisoners-library

Age-Specific Guidance

Caring for Children of Incarcerated Parents

http://nrccfi.camden.rutgers.edu/files/cipl201-caringforcip.pdf

Advice for Caregivers

Questions from Caregivers

http://nrccfi.camden.rutgers.edu/files/cipl202-questionsfromcaregivers.pdf

Tips from Caregivers for Caregivers
http://nrccfi.camden.rutgers.edu/files/cpl204-tipsfromcaregivers.pdf

The New Jersey Department of Corrections
"What about me?" When a parent goes to prison: A guide to discussing your incarceration with your children
www.state.nj.us/corrections/pdf/OTS/InmateFamilyResources/WhatAboutMe.pdf
Preparing children for prison visits.

The Oregon Program
"Parenting Inside Out"
www.parentinginsideout.org
www.parentinginsideout.org/resources
An evidence-based curriculum for incarcerated mothers and fathers, including a set of materials targeted toward educators and caregivers and a collection of resources for children.

Sesame Street
Little Children, Big Challenges: Incarceration
www.sesamestreet.org/toolkits/incarceration
A series of online toolkits for children and their parents dealing with adversity. Issues include not just prison, but also bullying, divorce, and relocation. The toolkit contains videos, activities, and handouts offering advice, encouragement, and games for when they visit Mom or Dad in jail.

Youth.gov
Children of Incarcerated Parents
http://youth.gov/youth-topics/children-of-incarcerated-parents
For more information and resources on these overlapping problems, please see the additional links and resources at this site.

PUBLICATIONS

We suggest exploring the Internet and public libraries for books about children with an incarcerated parent.

Barnes-Robinson, L. and Jeweler, S. (2007). Conflict resolution: Teaching Conflict Resolution and Mediation through the Curriculum. Hawthorne, NJ: Educational Impressions, Inc.

Bouchet, S.M. (2008). Children and Families with Incarcerated Parents. Annie E. Casey Foundation.

Christian, S. (2009). Children of Incarcerated Parents. National Conference of State Legislatures.

Correia, M.E. "Determinants of attitudes toward police of Latino immigrants and non-immigrants." Retrieved October 13, 2010. http://www.sciencedirect.com/science?_ob=ArticleURL&udi=B6V

Gable, S. (1992). "Children of incarcerated and criminal parents: Adjustment, behavior, and prognosis." Bull Am Acad Psychiatry Law, 20 (1), 89-113.

Glaze, L.E. and Maruschak, L.M. (2008). Parents in Prison and Their Children. U.S. Department of Justice, Bureau of Justice Statistics. Washington, DC: Government Printing Office.

Hairston, C.F. (2007). Focus on Children with Incarcerated Parents. Annie E. Casey Foundation.

Jucovy, L. (2003). Amachi: Mentoring Children of Prisoners in Philadelphia. Philadelphia, PA: Public/Private Ventures.

La Vigne, N.G. (2008). Broken Bonds: Understanding and Addressing the Needs of Children with Incarcerated Parents. Annie E. Casey Foundation.

Montgomery County Public Schools (1994). Conflict Resolution Tools: Elementary Version, Teaching Through the Curriculum. Rockville, MD: Author.

Mumola, C.J. (2000). Bureau of Justice Statistics Special Report: Incarcerated Parents and Their Children. Washington, DC: U.S. Department of Justice [NCJ 182335].

Mumola, C.J. (2002). "1996 Survey of Inmates in Local Jails, 1997 Survey of Inmates in State and Federal Correctional Facilities, 2001 Annual Survey of Jails, and 2001 National Prisoners Statistics Program." (Presented at the National Center for Children and Families, Washington, DC, October 31, 2002.)

Nickel, J., Garland, C. and Kane, L. (2009). Children of Incarcerated Parents: An Action Plan for Federal Policymakers. New York: Council of State Governments Justice Center.

Parke, R. and Clarke-Stewart, K. A. (2002). "Effects of parental incarceration on young children." (Paper prepared for the "From Prison to Home" conference.)

Petras, D. D., Derozotes, D. M. and Wills, S. (1999). Parent-Child Bonding and Attachment: Research Implications for Child Welfare Practice. Dialogues on Child Welfare Issues. Chicago, IL: University of Illinois at Chicago, Jane Addams Center for Social Policy and Research.

Ramiro, M. (2007). "Incorporating Latinos and immigrants into policing research." Criminology & Public Policy, 6 (1), 57–64.

Resources and interventions for children of incarcerated parents. (2008). Baltimore, MD. University of Maryland School of Social Work.

Zimmer, J.A. (1998). Let's Say: "We can work it out!" Problem Solving Through Mediation Ages 8–13. Culver City, CA: Social Studies School Service.